SEA
SURVIVOR'S
GUIDE

SEA SURVIVOR'S GUIDE

Rory Storm

Illustrated by Mei Lim

SCHOLASTIC INC.

New York Toronto London Auckland Sydney
Mexico City New Delhi Hong Kong Buenos Aires

ISBN 0-439-32857-8

12 11 10 9 8 7 6 5 4 3 2 1   2 3 4 5 6 7/0

Printed in the U.S.A.   40
First Scholastic printing, February 2002

CONTENTS

WARNING!

This guide is to learn about extreme survival situations. The techniques are not suitable for use at home and are only to be used in real emergencies.

Rory

SO YOU WANNA SURVIVE AT SEA?

SO YOU WANNA SURVIVE AT SEA?

Can you recall the time in your life when you were the most scared? For me, it was in a raging storm on a tall ship in the Atlantic Ocean. The waves were crashing over the decks, the wind was howling, and I was sure we were going to capsize. Perhaps it wasn't the most dangerous situation of my survival career (after all, there have been a few tricky moments), but it was the moment at which I felt the most scared.

You see, like most soldiers, I felt out of my depth (no pun intended) at sea. It was an unfamiliar and forbidding environment and I felt helpless and at the mercy of the elements — not a nice feeling for a survival expert.

Since that occasion, I have been on many operations at sea, I've learned a lot, and I now have a great love of the oceans as well as a healthy respect for them. The sea can be a tranquil, calming, and reenergizing environment, but in a moment it can change to become a savage and ruthless adversary hell-bent on your destruction.

TOUGH ENVIRONMENT

In terms of survival, the sea has to be the toughest challenge of all. Without some sort of buoyancy aid, our survival time in the water can be measured in hours rather than days, but with a life raft and armed with courage and determination, survivors have been known to last for months.

That is why all ships' crews, marines, and Special Boat Service personnel are trained repeatedly in emergency procedures — simply because the marine environment is such a difficult and alien place in which to survive. But survive you must and with some of the skills you'll pick up in this book, you, too, will have a better chance of being a survivor at sea if the situation ever arises.

WHAT IT TAKES

Perhaps it is because we recognize the awesome power of the sea and because of our vulnerability in this environment that nautical explorers and adventurers have captured the public's imagination throughout the ages.

The latest in a long line of nautical heroes is 24-year-old Ellen MacArthur, who, from 2000–2001, single-handedly sailed nonstop around the world to come in second in the Vendée Globe race. She made international headlines, and we all admired her tenacity and courage in the face of great danger and adversity.

So, let's agree that those are two of the qualities that are obviously essential if you are to be a survivor at sea. But can you think of any others? Well, I hope you included inner strength, determination, and resilience on your list of personal attributes. Oh, and being able to swim helps but, believe it or not, it's not essential.

CHAPTER ONE

The most valuable qualities in a survivor at sea are a resourceful and innovative nature. Being able to improvise to make or repair essential equipment is the only way to survive in this corrosive environment.

Take for instance the story of a survivor from a shrimp trawler, which sank in April 1963 off Australia. As the trawler went down, a 7 ft x 8 ft (2.1 m x 2.4 m) icebox bobbed to the surface next to the skipper, Jack Drinan. He broke a hole in one of the 3-ft (0.9-m) compartments and spent the next twelve days afloat in it. For water, he licked the moisture from the icebox lid, spending his days bailing salt water from the craft with his shirt. Finally, he made a flimsy raft from the lid and, leaving the icebox "mother ship," he set out for shore. He survived by ingenuity and quick thinking, wouldn't you agree? As in all survival situations, the right attitude of mind and mental tenacity are the keys to staying alive.

ALL MOD CONS

Of course, sailing is safer now than it has ever been thanks to the latest innovations in weather forecasting, navigation, signaling, and survival equipment. But sometimes, it is plain common sense together with today's technology that saves the day.

In the case of Rebecca Fife, a British tourist on vacation in Indonesia, this was definitely true. She and 17 others, including tourists and crew, found themselves drifting dangerously in a stranded boat in the Lombok Straits after both engines on their 23-ft (7-m) pleasure craft failed. Unable to get in touch with local emergency services, the 19-year-old backpacker had the presence of mind to send a text message to her boyfriend, 8,000 miles (12,875 km) away in a bar in London.

When he read the message "Call Falmouth Coastguard — we need help — SOS," he telephoned her back and quickly got all the details because her cell phone battery was running low. After receiving Nick Hodgson's call, members of the British Coast Guard contacted their colleagues in Australia who, in turn, contacted Rebecca.

The stranded boat was then found by Indonesian rescuers and, although the 18 people couldn't be transferred due to the 14-ft (4.25-m) waves buffeting the craft, they were towed back to port and to safety.

The Coast Guard figured Rebecca had done exactly the right thing since she couldn't speak the local language, and this is also a great example of how modern technology can prove to be a lifesaver in survival situations — as long as you keep a cool head.

WHAT TO EXPECT

In *Sea Survivor's Guide*, we look at ways to provide yourself with the lifesaving essentials of staying afloat and getting drinking water so you can endure the harsh conditions you'll find at sea. You'll also want to avoid the many dangers that are constantly lurking in the waters, so we'll explore tactics for dealing with anything from abandoning ship and making a buoyancy aid to ways to prevent attacks from sharks and other predators.

Once you've tucked these basic survivor's skills under your life jacket, you'll have an opportunity to read about the brave souls who have had to employ these techniques for real. The courageous stories of real-life marine survivors plus the valiant tales of rescues at sea will definitely inspire you, and who knows . . . you may even pick up enough tricks along the way to help answer the "what if" scenarios later in the book.

And just when you thought it was safe to go back in the water, there's another chance to exercise your "little gray cells" with the Sea Survivor's Brainteasers. Here, you're invited to come up with your very own survival plan to save you and your companions from a watery grave.

MAN OVERBOARD

Finally, you can have every survival skill known to humankind under your belt, but if you don't have luck on your side your chances are limited. Let's end with the tale of one lucky survivor who definitely had someone watching over him.

In 1995, Zachary Mayo, a marine on the USS *America* came on deck to get some fresh air one night. Suddenly, the door swung open and knocked him 30 ft (9.1 m) into the sea. He watched helplessly as his ship sailed away leaving him alone and defenseless in the middle of the Indian Ocean. Can you just imagine the thoughts running through his head at this point?

Thinking quickly, Zachary kicked off both his boots and took off his trousers. He tied the legs into knots under the water and filled the legs up with air and then used them as a raft. (See page 24 to find out how to do this for yourself.)

Zachary kept reinflating his makeshift raft as he waited through the night, all the next day, and through the following night, bobbing alone in the vast ocean.

Meanwhile back on board the USS *America*, his absence wasn't noticed for 30 hours — and then, a search boat was immediately launched but they didn't find poor Zachary.

Eventually, on the second day, Zachary's prayers were answered and he was picked up, sunburned and exhausted, by a Pakistani fishing boat. A chance in a million — and one very lucky marine!

So let's hope that you, too, are blessed with good fortune and we'll get under way, okay? Full steam ahead!

ARE YOU A SURVIVOR AT SEA?

ARE YOU A SURVIVOR AT SEA?

Before we get down to the nitty-gritty of survival skills and to the amazing real-life stories of spectacular escapes and rescues, I thought it would be fun (well, for me, anyway) to start with a survival questionnaire.

Don't get upset about it though — it's simply to get an idea of just how much survival savvy you have at the outset. And whatever results you get now, I'll bet my bottom dollar that you'll be getting top marks by the end of this book.

So let's find out whether you're still a wet-behind-the-ears puddle pup or a salty old sea dog, okay?

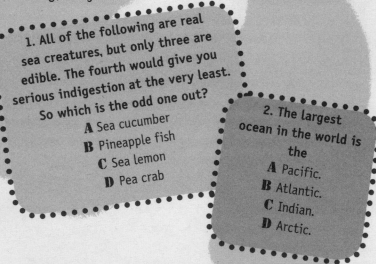

1. All of the following are real sea creatures, but only three are edible. The fourth would give you serious indigestion at the very least. So which is the odd one out?

A Sea cucumber
B Pineapple fish
C Sea lemon
D Pea crab

2. The largest ocean in the world is the
A Pacific.
B Atlantic.
C Indian.
D Arctic.

3. Your ship is sinking and you have to throw yourself into the sea. Should you:
A dive headfirst?
B jump feetfirst?
C star jump?
D belly flop?

4. In days of old, pirates used to wear gold earrings
A because they thought it made them look pretty.
B so the body could be identified if they died in battle.
C to draw attention away from the eyepatch.
D to improve their eyesight.

5. From what is coral made?
A Rocks
B Animals
C Plants
D Bones

6. Seawater covers what percentage of the earth's surface?
A 10 percent
B 30 percent
C 50 percent
D 70 percent

7. After being shipwrecked, you are floating in the water awaiting rescue when a shark starts to circle you. You should:
A splash the water to scare it away.
B minimize movement and remain calm.
C shoot it.
D throw up.

8. The largest animal on earth is a sea mammal. It is
A the blue whale.
B the humpback whale.
C the killer whale (orca).
D the sperm whale.

9. Giant tidal waves triggered by earthquakes or volcanoes beneath the sea are known as:
A currents.
B rollers.
C teriyaki.
D tsunamis.

10. A rescue helicopter arrives at your life raft and the winch operator sends down a harness. Who should be lifted to safety first?
A Women and children
B You
C The injured
D The ship's cat

11. The country with the most coastline is:
A Greenland.
B Canada.
C Switzerland.
D Indonesia.

12. The line drawn on the side of a ship showing how low the ship can safely sink when loaded in different water conditions is known as the:
A pump line.
B sneaker liner.
C Plimsoll line.
D sock line.

ANSWERS

So, was it a cinch or a complete nightmare? Let's find out. Award yourself one point for each correct answer.

1c Rather you than me, old buddy. A sea lemon is a type of sea slug, which squirts burning acid when disturbed. That's how they get their bitter name. All the rest are quite yummy, actually.

2a The Pacific is the world's biggest ocean, covering an area of 64 million square miles (166 million square km) — that's roughly one-third of the earth's surface, would you believe!

3b Always jump into the water in an upright position, with your legs crossed at the ankles just before entry. You should never dive into unknown waters — there could be debris just below the surface and any of the other positions will hurt horrendously and should be avoided.

4d Strange but true. Our fearless bunch of marauders believed that gold earrings helped their vision. Not the sharpest cutlasses in the box, hmm!

5b It used to be thought that coral was made from plants, but we now know that tiny animals called polyps build reefs. Polyps are a little like jellyfish and they build hard cases to protect their squishy bodies from predators. The reef is made up of the empty cases once the polyps leave, but the colorful top layer is alive and should not be touched because it's so easy to damage.

6d Astonishing, isn't it? Nearly three-quarters of the world is covered by the sea. No wonder it's a hard place in which to find a person overboard.

7b Despite what you see in the movies, very few types of shark will actually attack. However, they are very inquisitive, so try not to resemble their normal food source. If you shoot it, the blood will attract other sharks and these will devour anything in the vicinity of the feeding frenzy, so it's not a good idea. It's probably quite understandable to throw up or pee when a large shark is swimming around you, but bodily waste is very attractive to sharks (weird creatures!) so try to control yourself, please.

8a The blue whale can grow to a length of over 99 ft (30 m) and can weigh up to 165 tons (136 + metric). That's bigger than the largest dinosaur! It can reach this vast size only because its body is supported by the water — on land, the weight of its body would crush the blue whale's internal organs.

9d Tsunamis (soo-NAH-mees), a Japanese word meaning "harbor waves," contain enough water to swamp a whole island. The largest ever measured was 278 ft (85 m) high — that's taller than the Statue of Liberty. Wow, some wave, huh! Teriyaki is a Japanese flavoring!

10c In an unassisted recovery, help the injured and sick into the harness and let them be rescued first. Leave the able-bodied until last — and that includes the cat! Only a sneaky rat would get out first and leave the sick or those less able to fend for themselves, so I sincerely hope you didn't vote for yourself or you'll have me to answer to!

11b Not only is Canada one of the biggest countries in the world, but it can boast the most coastline. It has a staggering 55,925 miles (90,000 km) of seashore, which is pretty impressive, really. Indonesia comes second with a mere 29,205 miles (47,000 km). Switzerland is landlocked, of course, so I hope you didn't vote for that!

12c Yep, the Plimsoll line is marked on all ships. And who voted for sock line — are you completely crazy?

SCORING

0-3 points:
Well, moving swiftly on . . . no, seriously, you didn't shine in this test, but by the end of the book, I'll bet you'll be getting straight A's.

4-8 points:
Not bad, huh! Definitely a bit of a natural, but some room for improvement, I'd say.

9-12 points:
Hail the conquering hero — what a star! But there's no time to rest on your seaweed laurels — there's work to be done.

And, since the saying goes

"Time and tide wait for no man,"

we'd better get a move on.

BASIC SEA SURVIVAL SKILLS

BASIC SEA SURVIVAL SKILLS

Isn't it comforting to know that the vast majority of ships and commercial aircraft are now furnished with well-equipped life rafts in case the worst should happen and you're ditched in the sea? These craft have all the essentials for survival packed in them, and, with good signaling equipment on board, you can hope to be picked up by a search-and-rescue team before too long.

However, even the most careful planning and preparation cannot make allowances for every eventuality, and both misfortune and error (or sometimes a combination of the two) can mean that there are still occasions when your survival at sea relies principally on your own initiative, courage, and strength of mind.

All these qualities are essential if you are to survive in the vastness of the world's tumultuous oceans, but the odds are more heavily tipped in your favor if you have some vital survival skills tucked under your life jacket, too. So, without further ado, let's get down to basics, shall we?

SURVIVAL AT SEA

If your ship or plane goes down at sea, you have to hope you're one of the lucky ones who gets a place in a life raft or lifeboat because this radically improves your chances of survival.

However, first things first. It may be that, for some reason, you have to abandon ship without a life raft. In this case, it's essential to know how to enter the water and what to do once you're immersed in order to keep yourself alive until you can reach a lifeboat or some other floating debris.

JUMPING INTO WATER

≋ If you can't climb down into the water, get as near to the surface as possible before you jump.

≋ Make sure your life jacket is securely tied around you but is not inflated in case it gets snagged on something as you jump.

≋ Make sure your landing area is free from debris or other people before you jump.

≋ Be careful to jump clear of any protrusions sticking out from the boat.

≋ Keep your body straight; cross your ankles and fold your arms.

≋ With one hand, cover your mouth and nose to stop seawater from rushing up your nose, then close your eyes and jump.

≈ Hold on tight to your life jacket with the other hand.

≈ Once in the water, flatten out into the breaststroke position so you surface more quickly.

≈ Inflate your life jacket.

≈ Move away from the ship or aircraft to ensure no one else jumps on top of you.

≈ If fuel covers the water, move upwind in case it ignites.

≈ Look for the nearest life raft or flotation aid, such as debris.

Sea Survivor's Tip

If you have to jump into water that is covered with burning oil, don't inflate your life jacket. Swim underwater as far as your lungs will take you. If you're not clear of the burning area but have to come up for air, surface hands first, splashing the water aside. Grab a quick breath, and then submerge again without delay. Repeat this until you're in safe water; then, and only then, inflate your life jacket.

Fact File
Research shows that if you are afloat in cold seawater 50°F (10°C) dressed only in light clothing, you will not survive for more than three hours. Loss of body heat is a serious problem for the survivor at sea, and it is proven that several layers of clothing and a life jacket that keeps the head above water can considerably prolong survival time. Surprisingly, although you'd think exercise would warm you up, swimming also increases loss of body heat — so avoid it unless you're trying to reach a specific destination, such as a lifeboat.

SURVIVAL IN THE WATER

Naturally, your chances of survival are much better in warmer water. However, if you are adrift in a cold sea, take a look at these top survival tips, which may help to keep you alive:

≋ First, don't abandon ship unless you're absolutely sure it's going to sink.

≋ Make sure you've got plenty of clothing on to help keep you warm.

≋ Always wear a life jacket — not only does it keep your head out of the cold water but it also allows you to float and conserve energy/body heat.

≋ Don't swim except to reach a specific destination. Even if you can see land, never swim against the tide. Bide your time.

≋ The cold water will make you feel sleepy — fight this or you will certainly drown. Boredom is equally dangerous so keep alert by doing simple sums or conundrums.

≋ If you need to attract attention, use the whistle on your life jacket or wave one arm.

≋ Floating in your life jacket in the fetal position can increase survival time by up to 50 percent. Pull your knees up to your chest; cross your arms either inside or around your knees and cross your ankles.

KEEPING AFLOAT

We've already seen how useful a life jacket can be, but if you don't have one, don't despair. A resourceful survivor always finds a way to help him- or herself and this procedure may just save your life.

≋ Take off your trousers and tightly knot each leg just above the ankle cuffs. (You'll have to tread water while you do this so perhaps you should practice this skill at the local pool!)

≋ Holding the waistband, swing the trousers over your head, catching as much air as possible before splashing the open waistband onto the water's surface.

≋ Twist the waistband closed to trap the air in the trouser legs.

≋ Put one inflated leg under each arm to help you float with your head out of the water. Or even place around the neck.

Fact File

In October 1998, Hurricane Mitch hit the Caribbean and a huge flood wave struck Laura Isabelle's house. She was swept out to sea and, as she got farther and farther from the shore, she managed to grab and cling on to a piece of driftwood and, finally, on to an uprooted tree.

The huge seas battered the log but Laura Isabelle grimly hung on. She stayed afloat on her log for six days before being picked up by a passing Royal Navy ship. Without her buoyancy aid, however unconventional it may have been, she would certainly have perished. So, use your imagination and scout around if you find yourself adrift in the ocean.

LIFE RAFT LIFE

My bet is that as a shrewd and wily survivor, you're going to find yourself in a life raft. And, if you do, your spirits should lift significantly because, as survival situations go, you're now one step ahead of the game.

So, having checked that your raft is seaworthy and fully inflated, you can turn your immediate attention to checking the water for any other survivors and helping them aboard. Sometimes this is easier said than done, but the following pointers should improve your chances of success:

〰 **Most life rafts are equipped with a rescue quoit (ring) on a line, which can be thrown to swimmers to help them aboard.**

〰 **If the survivor is unable to catch the quoit, then a strong swimmer should use the safety line to go into the water and recover them.**

〰 **Once the raft is full, the able-bodied among you should tend to the needs of the injured or sick. This will probably mean preventing hypothermia in cold seas (see page 88).**

RESCUE

So, you're snug in your life raft and awaiting rescue. Job done, you may think. Well, that's where you'd be wrong. You can't just sit back and wait for others to come and find you. For a start, it may take longer than you imagine, and, more to the point, there's a lot you can do to help yourself, too.

It may be hours or it may be days before you're picked up, so right from the start get into the good habit of implementing a survival routine. The following are just some of the tasks that need to be carried out regularly:

≋ Search for other survivors.

≋ Set up a radio or beacon.

≋ Check the raft for seaworthiness and carry out repairs where necessary.

≋ Top off the air in the raft.

≋ Check the sea anchor.

≋ Station a lookout (two hours on, four hours off is what I'd recommend) and make sure everyone is familiar with how to use the signaling equipment.

≋ Maintain the seawater pump or solar still.

≋ Ration out the food and water.

≋ Set up fishing lines.

Sea Survivor's Tip

Make sure you use the sea anchor provided to stop drifting. Amazingly, your position can change by 50-80 miles (80-130km) per day by drifting. A sea anchor will keep you closer to your last reported position and so help rescuers. If you don't have a proper sea anchor, a bucket hanging under the life raft on a rope, or even some bulky clothing, does a similar job.

FOOD AND DRINK

So, here you are, bobbing around on the ocean waves with no land for hundreds of miles and no sign of rescue. What are you going to do?

Well, unless you're extremely unfortunate, your life raft should provide you with the shelter you need to stay alive indefinitely. So now you need to turn your attention to sustenance. And since a large burger and fries is out of the question, perhaps you'd better look at what the ocean can offer.

Fishing is the obvious choice and life raft survival kits are usually equipped with some tackle. If not, you can always improvise — Marilyn Bailey fished very successfully during her family's 117 days adrift using a safety pin for a hook!

As well as fish, seabirds are also a good source of nutrition, but take it from me, they taste pretty awful. That said, beggars can't be choosers, and if you leave a baited hook and get a catch, you'll be grateful for the meal, however unpalatable.

You'll find emergency rations in the survival pack but these should be reserved for the days when you don't get a catch. In the meantime, think like Huckleberry Finn and see what you can do with your hook and line:

≈ **Be very careful when handling fishing tackle. Not only can it cut you very easily, but it can puncture the rubber raft, spelling disaster.**

≈ **Don't fish if sharks are in the vicinity.**

≈ **Take care when landing large fish because they can also damage the raft. If a fish is proving particularly tricky to land, cut it loose rather than risk a danger to the raft.**

≈ **Gut and bleed any fish you catch immediately, and use the entrails for bait.**

≈ **Cut fish into thin slices and eat raw (if you're squeamish, remind yourself that you'd pay a fortune for this in a Japanese restaurant!). Any leftovers can be hung up to dry — air-dried fish can last for up to a week.**

〰 Avoid fish that are spiny, boxlike, or oddly shaped, and avoid jellyfish.

〰 Don't eat any fish that has sunken eyes, looks slimy, or stinks to high heaven.

Sea Survivor's Tip

If you clean your catch with a knife, make sure you fold the blade away when not in use to avoid accidents. A knife is a precious commodity that you cannot afford to lose, so secure knives to your clothing or to the boat to stop them from going overboard.

Fact File

The phrase "booby trap" comes from the sailors' custom of putting a loop of string around a piece of bait to catch the Booby bird. Apparently, these large seabirds are a little dumb and very easy to catch.

WATER, WATER, EVERYWHERE, BUT NOT A DROP TO DRINK

Strangely enough, food is not your highest priority during a survival ordeal at sea. Nice though it is to eat, you'll find that since you're not moving around much in a life raft, you don't need many calories to keep going. But there is one thing that is essential to your survival. Can you guess what it is?

Yep, top marks to all those who said drinking water. And, ironically, this is hard to come by in the vast expanses of our salty seas. A modern life raft should provide you with equipment for converting seawater into drinkable water, but even with such devices, water remains an essential to life. So you must conserve body fluids and ration any reserves of drinking water, particularly in hot, tropical oceans.

CONSERVING BODY FLUIDS

≋ Improvise to make some kind of sun shade.

≋ If not, wet your clothing in the sea to cool the body if you find yourself directly under the tropical sun.

≋ Rest and sleep during the day.

≋ Don't overdo it — conserve energy.

EQUIPMENT

A seawater pump will take the salt out of the seawater and make it drinkable (called potable in seafaring circles). It can produce about 2 pints (1 liter) of potable water an hour — not bad, huh? And not only does it desalinate, but it removes all bacteria and viruses, too.

The next best thing to a seawater pump is a solar still. This has a clear plastic dome-shaped top and an inflatable base. Seawater is poured into one compartment and due to the strength of the sun's rays, this is distilled into freshwater and collected in a separate compartment. A solar still can also be used to purify urine.

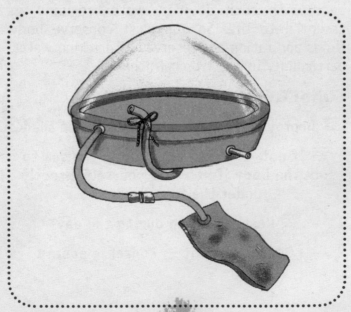

CHAPTER THREE

NATURE'S SUPPLY

We shouldn't forget the most obvious source of drinking water. Can you hazard a guess as to what I mean? Of course, it's rainwater. Keep an eye open for gathering rain clouds and be ready to catch as much rain as possible during a downpour. You can stretch out some sheeting, a sail, or a foil blanket to catch as much as possible. Fill any receptacles you have — you can even fill up the solar still's containers.

Use clean, spare clothing to soak up the rain and then wring it out into pots — and once you've filled every conceivable container, start drinking your fill.

As long as you're in a warm climate, you can also take this opportunity for a welcome wash and scrub up. Wash all the salt off your body and rinse out any clothing that is soaked in seawater.

Sea Survivor's Tip

It doesn't matter how thirsty you become, you must NEVER drink seawater or urine. If you do, this will cause kidney failure and madness and you will certainly die more quickly than if you drink no water at all. It's a horrific way to go, so just make sure you resist the temptation.

SEA RESCUE

Right then. You've got your shelter, food, and water sorted out. What's left?

Well, how do you figure a plane searching in acres and acres of open sea is going to find little old you? Got it in one. Signaling, of course. I'm sure you're sensible enough to use the radio beacons or radar reflectors that you'll find in the life raft from the moment you get yourself out of the water. But there are also other ways in which you can draw attention to yourself and your fellow survivors.

≋ **If there are several life rafts floating around, lash them together to form a larger target for the SAR (search-and-rescue) aircraft to spot.**

≋ **The same applies if you are in the water with only a life jacket — stick together and you're more conspicuous — it may sound funny but a human "conga" line or circle gives you a much better chance of being spotted.**

≋ **Constantly use the heliograph (a specially designed reflector) or a mirror to scan the horizon.**

≋ **At night, if you hear engines, use a flashlight to signal.**

≋ Only use flares if they stand a very good chance of being spotted, i.e., the rescue craft is nearby, because they can only be used once.

≋ If you reach land, make a driftwood signal fire on the beach.

≋ Mark out a permanent distress code on the sand and make it big and contrasting to the sand.

≋ If a search aircraft finds you, it may simply drop you supplies and return sometime later once a rescue can be organized — don't despair: The crew will have noted your location.

≋ Once a rescue helicopter arrives, follow the instructions given by the winch operator. Keep calm and wait patiently. I know it's hard, but it is safer for all concerned.

ALL CLEAR

So, after a close shave, you're safe once again. Now let's move on and find out how some other people coped in the savage seas when they met disaster in our oceans for real.

SURVIVORS IN ICY WATERS

SURVIVORS IN ICY WATERS

The cold is a killer. This much we know. So, imagine being exposed to bitingly cold temperatures together with monstrous waves, which seem bent on destroying you and your boat. This is the situation that faced all of the following survivors who each showed extreme courage, endurance, and determination in the face of seemingly insurmountable odds.

Their stories are mesmerizing, all the more so because they are true. As you settle down to read and enjoy these adventures, put yourself in their shoes for a moment and just try to imagine what it must be like to face such savage seas.

FIGHT FOR LIFE IN THE ICY DEPTHS

In 1996, an expedition to the magnetic South Pole, which lies 80 nautical miles (148 km) off the coast of Antarctica, was mounted under the leadership of David Hempleman-Adams. A young Australian named Pete Bland was a crew member but there was no way that he could have known at the start of the trip what a pivotal role he was going to play in saving the lives of his fellow crewmates.

MILES FROM HELP

The *Spirit of Sydney* had entered the iceberg-strewn waters of the southern seas and they knew it would take at least five or six days for the nearest ship to reach them if they ran into difficulties. It was at this distant point that a rope fell over the side of the ship and became wrapped around the propeller, crippling the ship.

The expedition was now reduced to using a sail to navigate through the treacherous icebergs where speed is absolutely essential to get through successfully. The crew knew it was only a matter of time before disaster, in the form of a towering iceberg, struck the ship.

They tried desperately for five days to free the rope, even reversing the engine but this simply ensnared the prop still further. Can you imagine how frustrating and nerve-racking that wait must have been?

CERTAIN DEATH

Eventually, they decided that the rope had to be cut and called for a volunteer. Yep, you've guessed it — Pete Bland put up his hand. The doctor explained that none of them could endure more than a maximum of five minutes in these icy waters, particularly since they had no wetsuit or scuba equipment. Many believed this to be a suicide mission, but Pete still agreed to go.

The water temperature was 30.2°F (-1°C) and the air temperature was -76°F (-60°C)! Pete was attached to a rope and, armed with a sharp knife, he lowered himself into the water. He dived down about 12 ft (3.6 m) and started cutting for all he was worth. Repeatedly he came up for breath and then dived again.

He was so cold that his brain didn't function properly and he couldn't even get the words out to ask for more slack in the rope.

DANGER WARNING

By now, Pete had been in the water four and a half minutes and he was perilously close to death. However, he dived once again and cut furiously until he heard metal on metal and realized he'd gotten through the high-stress rope.

Pete was dragged from the water and, by rights, he should have been dead. Miraculously, he lived to tell the tale and the expedition continued on to the magnetic South Pole. Now, it takes a certain sort of courage to consciously put your life on the line to save your fellow sailors, and, I think you'll agree, Pete Bland had bravery in spades. However, he paid a price.

SHOCKING NEWS

On his return to Australia, he collapsed with an aortic aneurysm, and he could have died at any moment. He was taken to the hospital and the surgeon replaced the damaged vessel with an artificial tube. The doctors explained that Pete's Antarctic dive had exacerbated a slight weakness in his heart.

Undaunted, Pete was determined to recover fully so that he could get back to extreme adventuring. True to his word, he joined an expedition to the magnetic North Pole in 1998.

Sadly, it wasn't successful, but Pete is still determined to be the first Australian to reach both magnetic poles. He now uses his expeditions to raise money and awareness for heart disease — a remarkable man, don't you agree?

Fact File
You should never walk on frozen lakes or rivers because you could go through the ice. If you're dumb enough or unfortunate enough to find yourself on ice and it starts to crack, lie down. This spreads the weight, and, like this, you can inch your way back to safety. Putting all your weight through one foot as you run toward solid ground exerts enormous force on the ice and is likely to send you crashing through into the icy waters below.

SINGLE-HANDED SURVIVAL

Every four years, about twenty intrepid sailors set out to single-handedly sail nonstop around the world. As if this were not crazy enough, they are actually racing against one another, and the race is called the Vendée Globe.

CHAPTER FOUR

In February 2001, the triumphant face of Ellen MacArthur, the runner-up, was splashed all over the newspapers, but the outstanding images of the previous race in January 1997, were very, very different.

The 1996/97 racers were hit by deadly storm systems in the Antarctic Ocean, and the abiding images are of Thierry Dubois clinging to the keel and rudder of his upturned boat, and Tony Bullimore being rescued after three days trapped inside his capsized hull!

MONSTER WAVES

Despite Bullimore's twenty-seven Atlantic crossings, nothing could have prepared him for the weather in the Antarctic Ocean. At one point, Bullimore thought he'd seen an iceberg, but on second glance, he realized that he was witnessing a rogue wave eight stories high! Just imagine that.

This monster wave was rolling toward Bullimore's small boat, just looking for something to slow it down. And it wasn't alone. Sixty-foot (18-m) waves were rolling in from two directions, colliding and sending spray 100 ft (30 m) into the air. The sea was whipped into a white frenzy and the wind-speed indicator nudged 70 knots.

Bullimore's yacht could not withstand the pummeling and a vast wave flipped it over, with Bullimore trapped inside in a small pocket of air.

It was pitch-black and freezing cold. He was alone and 2,500 miles (4,000 km) south of Australia, the nearest inhabited land. So just how frightened do you think he must have felt?

Tony Bullimore is remarkable for his bravery and resourcefulness. He stayed like this for three days, tapping on the hull of his ship to announce his presence. He was eventually rescued by the Australian Navy.

On being pulled to safety, Bullimore was so relieved that he kissed the burly sailor who pulled him free from his crippled yacht. Steady buddy, you might think, but, in the circumstances, I think this was a perfectly natural reaction from one brave and grateful man to another.

WREAKING HAVOC

Meanwhile, the same storm had hit Thierry Dubois's *Amnesty pour International* with winds of 65 knots and more. Twice his yacht was knocked down with its mast in the water. The third time, it somersaulted completely and the mast broke.

Despite the extreme conditions, Dubois calmly set about trying to work out how to jury-rig a new mast. Unfortunately, without its tall mast, the race boat was very unstable and twice more during the three-day tempest, it was rolled by a huge wave. What must have been going through the young Frenchman's mind at this point?

The second time, the 60-ft (18-m) yacht stayed

upside down, and Dubois had to cling to the upturned keel until, with great good fortune because he was thousands of miles from land, he, too, was rescued.

SELFLESS ACT

As if all that weren't enough, Dinelli, another Vendée Globe competitor, was simultaneously being rescued by Pete Goss, a fellow racer, just an hour before his boat sank some 2,000 miles (3,200 km) farther east. The mountainous seas and fierce winds made Goss's task of backtracking for the stricken sailor a superhuman effort. Pretty selfless, huh?

This was a remarkably eventful race, and all of the competitors are enormously courageous to even take on such an event. So, would you be surprised to learn that all are still sailing and that Dubois and Dinelli took part in this year's Vendée Globe? No, I guess not. That's just the sort of caliber of men these guys are.

> **Fact File**
> **Waves the size of buildings!**
> One in every 300,000 waves will exceed the average wave size by four times. So if you're sailing in 10-ft (3-m) seas, you've got a one in 300,000 chance of a monster 40-ft (12-m) wave (the size of a house) crashing down on you. Of course, the average size of a wave in the vastness of the Antarctic Ocean is considerably bigger than other seas, so this, together with the freak weather systems experienced that far south, caused the monster waves that gave the Vendée Globe contestants so much grief!

SURVIVAL IN FROZEN WATERS

Elmo Wortman and his four children lived a secluded life near the town of Craig in northern Alaska. This small castaway community was far removed from any city comforts, and they lived off the land in a remote, harsh environment.

A trip to the dentist meant sailing 180 miles (290 km) over some of the roughest water in North America, to Prince Rupert in British Columbia, then driving 96 miles (155 km) inland to the clinic.

CHAPTER FOUR

Fact File
In the 1989/90 and the 1992/93
Vendée Globe solo events, 13
boats started each time, and only
half that number finished.

DISASTER STRIKES

On February 13, 1979, Elmo was returning home with his family, Jena, aged 12, Randy, 15, and Cindy, 16, after a trip to the dentist. (Margery, the eldest child, was staying with friends.) Elmo Wortman had the flu and was in his bunk — Jena was at the wheel of the boat when the storm struck.

For 30 hours their yacht withstood the battering 80-mph (128-kph) winds and massive seas, but near midnight on February 14, the yacht foundered. The dinghy, which they had packed with survival provisions, was washed away and they had to abandon ship.

Although Elmo was knocked unconscious, miraculously, they all survived.

A HASTY SHELTER

Washed up on the shore of a deserted coastline, they now needed protection from the harsh winds.

They made a crude shelter and started a fire —

amazingly, Randy still had some dry matches. They went beachcombing and managed to find a few apples and some mussels, and by a stroke of luck, the empty dinghy was also washed ashore.

Elmo worked out their approximate location and estimated that a cabin he knew of was no more than 25 miles (40 km) away. From there, he thought they could hitch a boat ride, and get home safely.

That night they rested in their makeshift shelter but the wind and snow made for an uncomfortable night's rest. The next morning, they patched together the damaged dinghy and Randy and Jena (it could only hold two) started to paddle along the coast. Meanwhile, Elmo and Cindy clambered along the cliff tops and made their way as best they could on foot. The going was very tough and cold, and they had to follow the shore around each deep inlet.

Finally, they reached Randy and Jena, waiting for them in a small cove.

RAFT-BUILDING

Dozens of logs lay strewn along the beach so they decided to make a raft. Amazingly, it floated and they paddled off. The raft was soon caught in the full force of the wind and waves, and, with everyone soaked in freezing water, they had to turn back and wait for better weather.

That night, they set off again, taking turns to row. At dawn, the wind finally forced them ashore where they were stranded for another day. Once again, they boarded the raft but were beaten landward by strong currents. The little inlet where they landed was covered in more than 2 ft (0.6 m) of snow and was extremely exposed.

Looking along the shore, Elmo could see what he believed to be Rose Inlet, where the cabin was located, only 3 miles (5 km) away. Immediately, he decided that he and Randy should leave the girls on the shore and paddle the dinghy to the cabin to raise the alarm.

LEAVING THE GIRLS BEHIND

As he said good-bye, Elmo was aware that the girls had no food and no means of making a fire in this bleak wilderness. He promised they would be back in three hours. He left his daughters huddled under a sail on the beach.

However, they were mistaken — it was not Rose Inlet they'd seen, but there was no turning back.

The three hours in which they promised to return had long since passed. Eventually, the mouth to Rose Inlet came into view but night was falling and Randy was exhausted. They could see the cabin about 50 ft (15 m) above the high-water mark but the inlet was covered in sea ice, which forced them to walk the last mile.

They used the last vestiges of their energy to cross the ice — Elmo even fell in at one point — and when they finally reached the cabin, they collapsed with exhaustion.

They discovered, to their despair, that the radio was broken; in the morning Elmo repaired it and transmitted a Mayday message but there was no response. Both men were experiencing excruciating pain as their frostbitten flesh started to thaw out.

ICY WAIT

Meanwhile, the girls were still huddled under the sail on the exposed beach. They had eaten bits of seaweed and sucked snow for water. They resorted to singing and reciting the Lord's Prayer to give themselves some comfort.

Elmo and Randy felt sure that the girls must, by now, be dead. Not that they could move to rescue the girls anyway, because of their swollen limbs and the extreme weather conditions.

At last, on the 12th day after they had split up, the weather changed. Overnight, the snow and ice melted, the wind changed direction, and it started to rain.

Elmo and Randy launched a leaky motorboat hull they'd found and with one bailing while the other rowed, they set out to collect the girls' bodies. Leaving a note for the cabin owners, they took two sleeping bags and enough food for four days.

It was now three and a half weeks since the shipwreck and nearly 15 days since the girls had been left on their own. Suddenly, the girls awoke to hear, "My babies, I've come back to get my babies," and lifted the sail to see their father.

SALVATION

Elmo could not believe they were still alive. Randy heard the commotion and came hobbling up the beach to see his sisters and join in the remarkable reunion. The girls had to be carried to the boat where they were wrapped in the sleeping bags. The family reached the cabin after dark. In the meantime, the owner had returned and, on reading Elmo's note, had left fresh groceries for them and went for help.

The next morning, they heard the sound of the helicopter and their ordeal was over.

Elmo Wortman lost half his right foot and all the toes on his left foot, and Cindy lost some toes. The girls said that they believed unwaveringly that their father would come back for them and that's what kept them going.

Now that's what I call indomitable spirit!

SURVIVING IN SHARK-INFESTED SEAS

SURVIVING IN SHARK-INFESTED SEAS

It's fair to say that you stand a better chance of survival in warmer waters as long as you're picked up quickly. But, tropical seas and a balmy climate bring with them their very own set of problems.

Those who survive the perils of glaring heat, shark attacks, and debilitating thirst must have mental strength and tenacity, as well as physical courage and determination.

The following true stories show how easy it might be to give up hope in these circumstances, and just how tough you have to be to survive in shark-infested seas.

ADRIFT IN SHARK-INFESTED WATERS

A group of friends left Florida for the Bahamas on a two-masted, 60-ft (18-m) yacht, aptly named *The Trashman*. Halfway through their voyage, *The Trashman* sank in a ferocious storm. Debbie Scaling, an experienced sailor, and her four crewmates found themselves in a small inflatable life raft, in the middle of a raging ocean. They spent the first night in the water, under the upside-down inflatable, trying to keep warm.

In the morning, they discovered the water was teeming with sharks. It's a miracle that they weren't eaten that first night in the water, but they wasted no time getting into the dinghy after that.

RAGING THIRST

With no food, no water, and inadequate clothing, the survivors had to endure hideous sores, terrible hunger and thirst, and diving attacks from seabirds. Driven beyond endurance, two of the crew drank seawater and little by little, went crazy. With the others too weak to stop them, they swam off and didn't survive. The skipper's girlfriend, who had sustained nasty injuries during the shipwreck, also died — of exposure and gangrene. By this time, Debbie and her sole surviving crewmate, Brad, had resigned themselves to their fate at the mercy of the sea.

PLUCKED FROM THE JAWS OF DEATH

For five days and five nights the raft drifted on the open sea, circled by a school of sharks, before being picked up by a Russian ship. Even as they were being rescued, a huge wave threatened to pluck the survivors from the arms of their rescuers. They were very lucky indeed to be alive and to have survived the horrors of that voyage.

Fact File

An eight-year-old boy from Ocean Springs, Mississippi, was playing in knee-deep water at the Gulf Islands National Seashore, Florida, on July 6, 2001, when a shark attacked and bit off his right arm. The shark was shot dead and bystanders managed to retrieve the limb from the dead shark's jaws. Remarkably, surgeons were able to reattach Jessie Arbogast's arm.

Sea Survivor's Tip

Shark attacks usually result in severe shock, extreme loss of blood, and horrendous tearing of the flesh. The experts suggest the following treatment:

In the Water

- Get the victim to the shore as soon as possible.
- If a boat is available, use it.
- Apply direct pressure or constrictive bandaging to control bleeding as soon as the patient is brought to the boat.

On the Beach

- Carry the patient head down, above the waterline.
- Keep the head below the level of the feet if possible.
- Reassure the patient and keep him or her quiet and still.
- Press hard with fingers and hands on spurting blood vessels. Fill the wound firmly with clean handkerchiefs or any other clean material.
- Bandage tightly if necessary above the wound — ease off every 15 minutes, except in the case of a severed limb.
- Ask a bystander to get medical help immediately.
- Do not warm the patient — a light cover only is recommended — and just moisten the patient's mouth, but don't give food or drink.

ALONE IN THE OCEAN

In 1982, Steven Callahan's sloop, *Napoleon Solo*, sank six days out from the Canary Islands. He was left adrift in a 5.5-ft (1.6-m) inflatable raft with the few items he'd managed to grab as his boat went down: paddles, flares, a signal mirror, 6 pints (12 liters) of water, fishing kit, navigational equipment, solar stills, and his ditch kit. This was a Tupperware box containing 21 emergency flares, 3 lb (1.3 kg) of emergency food, a knife, pencils, 2 pints (4 liters) of water, and a speargun. He was certainly better prepared than most, but he was going to need every item since Steve eventually spent 76 days adrift on his own.

Initially, Callahan was extremely pessimistic. He knew he was in the middle of the Atlantic Ocean and his chances of rescue were remote. However, in his ditch kit was a book by Dougal Robertson about his family's survival-at-sea experience, and this proved to be enough inspiration to raise Callahan's spirits.

GETTING FOOD AND DRINK

He reckoned he had enough water to last 18 days but not enough to reach landfall, so Steve was very strict and limited himself to a sip every two hours — the wait was terrible. Steve hated the fact that he had to catch drinking water in the same box that he had to defecate in — but you do what you must when it is a survival situation.

He filled his time by setting up the solar still and trying to catch fish. It took him two weeks to catch his first fish, even with a speargun! When he caught his first Dorado — it was manna from heaven and Callahan was elated. The large eyes were a real treat because they were full of delicious fluid.

DASHED HOPES

It was about this time that Callahan spotted a single ship. He thought he was saved and, in jubilation, sent off flares and drank his remaining water supply — but the boat didn't notice him. This was probably one of the lowest points of his whole ordeal — could you have faced such bitter disappointment?

TOUGH REGIME

Callahan fell into an arduous routine of operating the still, fishing, bailing out after the frequent storms, and making repairs to the boat and equipment. He frequently had to fend off shark attacks with his spear. His daily yoga routine, which he introduced to stop his muscles atrophying, used to take him half an hour in the early days of his ordeal but ended up taking an exhausting hour and a half as he grew weaker.

On the 43rd day, he speared a large fish, but it broke his spear and ripped a hole in the bottom of the boat. This was extremely serious and threatened his whole survival.

Ingeniously, Callahan fashioned a kind of patch out of foam and rope lashing, but it needed constant attention and servicing, and, as if his routine had not been hard enough, he now had to bail more regularly.

NAVIGATION

Partly to occupy his time and partly because he knew his survival might depend upon it, Callahan was determined to work out his position, which he estimated to be about 600 miles (965 km) from the West Indies. He timed how long a piece of seaweed took to reach the end of a known length of rope and from this, he could calculate how far west he had traveled. He also made a primitive sextant to work out his longitudinal (north and south) position. Could you have been bothered to go to such lengths? Maybe not. But it was his determination and positive attitude that got Steve Callahan through his lonely ordeal.

LAND AHOY

On the 75th night, Callahan spotted a flashing light from a lighthouse. He knew he was close to land, and, sure enough, the following day he was finally rescued by local fishermen.

He had been adrift for two and a half months since his boat sank and he'd lost a third of his body weight, but during that time, despite some very low moments, Steve Callahan never gave up hope that he'd be rescued. More than that, he did everything in his power — and then some — to make sure of his own survival. A remarkable man and true survivor, don't you agree?

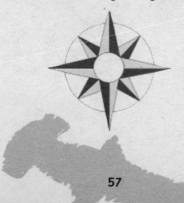

Sea Survivor's Tip

Even deserted terrain offers more survival resources than the open sea. So, if you reach an island or coastline, try to land. However, getting to land can be treacherous, so consider the following tips:

- Continue around the coast until you find a safe inlet.

- Avoid shores protected by cliffs.

- Beaching in strong surf is very dangerous — watch for breaks in the surf line and avoid hidden coral reefs by using your oars to steer.

- Avoid tropical shorelines that are muddy or thick with root formations, and search for a sand or pebble beach instead.

- In cold waters, avoid any ice floes with large ice cliffs above, since they often send large chunks crashing into the sea.

- If you land on a large floe, keep the raft inflated on the ice and use it as a shelter.

- Do not damage or discard your boat until you are sure you will not need it again.

CHAPTER FIVE

FIGHT FOR SURVIVAL

Robert Aros had always loved the sea. He learned to sail as a young man, and in 1980, he bought a 36-ft (11-m) wooden sloop called the *Vamonos* so that he could realize his dream of sailing around the South Pacific with his wife, Margaret, and son, Christian.

Aros was well prepared for the adventure ahead — he was an experienced sail racer and navigator, and he had an arsenal of survival, rescue, and first-aid skills learned in his role as part of the National Ski Patrol. However, Aros could not have known at the time just how essential these skills would prove to be.

DISASTER STRIKES

The family set off on their two-year dream tour but the dream turned into a nightmare when in November 1982, the *Vamonos* struck a remote reef between the Cook Islands and New Zealand, and sank.

For various reasons, the family could not take the life raft but found themselves adrift in a tiny rubber dinghy. For 26 harrowing days, the family floated helplessly on El Ninõ–churned seas, desperately low on food and water and without any way of steering their vessel.

A series of blunders and mistakes resulted in failed rescue attempts that plunged the family into despair — they began to believe that they could not survive their ordeal. It was faith and love that kept them together and grim determination that kept them alive until their eventual rescue.

Fact File
Shipwreck Endurance Record

Five fishermen from Costa Rica struggled in the immensity of the Pacific Ocean for an incredible 142 days, the longest such endurance on record. The ordeal began when a sudden storm overtook and sank their small fishing boat, Cairo III.

Later, they said that it was cooperation, perseverance, hope, and inner strength that saw the men through their ordeal. When finally rescued, they had drifted 4,500 miles (7,240 km) from their home shores, crossing four time zones, and had survived on a diet of rainwater, fish, and turtles. Amazing, huh?

One of the survivors said, "La esperanza es lo último que se pierde." ("Hope is the last thing you lose.")

WHALE ATTACK

Britons Maurice and Marilyn Bailey had always wanted to travel to New Zealand — by boat! And so the adventure started. . . .

All seemed to be going swimmingly well as they made their way across the Pacific to New Zealand. However, early one morning, all that was to change.

Suddenly, a 40-ft (12-m) sperm whale surfaced alongside their boat and, without any provocation, smashed its mighty tail down onto the hull. The boat immediately started to take on water and the Baileys knew it was only a matter of time before it would sink.

COOL-HEADED

The couple calmly collected together as many of the essentials as they could and put them in the life raft. However, as experienced sailors, they knew that the chances of rescue were slim. Yet, they were determined to remain optimistic.

Their supplies lasted for only ten days, but, ingeniously, they improvised some fishing tackle with a safety pin from the first-aid kit and some string, and, in this way, they managed to catch more than 4,000 fish during their ordeal.

Catching a shark for the first time made a sharp impression on Marilyn. She managed to catch the shark by its tail and held on for dear life. Soon, it stopped struggling (sharks drown if they don't keep moving). She then flopped it into the life raft and smothered its head with a towel — keeping well away from the sharp teeth.

With fish on the menu, the couple slaked their thirst with rainwater collected in the inflatable cover on their raft — pretty ingenious, I'd say.

OCEANIC DESERT

However, their luck was about to run out. The life raft drifted into a section of the ocean that was bereft of fish. They thought they were going to die of starvation or thirst (no rain, either!), and both had to face the unpalatable thought that the final survivor might have to consume the first who succumbed!

HIGH MORALE

Both Maurice and Marilyn are natural-born survivors and neither would allow their predicament to get them down. Day after day, as they continued to drift, they occupied themselves by planning their next boat and another voyage.

After 17 weeks adrift (119 days), Marilyn was roused from her reveries by the sound of a ship's engine. Shakily, the pair stood up and with what little strength they had left, they waved pieces of clothing as a signal. Feeling desperate, the Baileys watched as the ship appeared to steam on by, but, remarkably, the ship turned. It had seen them and rescue was imminent.

CHAPTER FIVE

SUCKERS FOR PUNISHMENT

The Baileys were taken to Honolulu for medical treatment, and two months later, they arrived back in England. And guess what was the first thing they did? You got it. They began to plan their next voyage. Incorrigible.

Sea Survivor's Tip
Dangerous Sea Creatures

Whales and Killer Whales:
These enormously powerful creatures are dangerous because they have been known to attack and sink small boats. A blow from their gigantic tails and it's "lights out" for you.

Sharks:
There are ways to avoid shark attacks (see pages 99–100), but only certain species are likely to attack you — though if you see a fin coming at you, I guess spotting the species might be low on your list of priorities.

Barracuda:
These tropical and sub-tropical fish grow to considerable lengths and are particularly aggressive — often attacking without provocation. Use the same precautions as for sharks.

Jellyfish:
These may not look like much but a jellyfish sting can be excruciatingly painful. The largest of all jellyfish, the Portuguese man-of-war has trailing tentacles that can cause shock and severe cramps that often lead to drowning. Avoid them like the plague.

Crocodiles:
Yes, surprising as it may seem, crocodiles often venture several miles from shore and are common in the mangrove swamps, estuaries, and saltwater bays of the East Indies and South-east Asia. So, keep your eyes peeled.

CHAPTER FIVE

Fact File
In June 1972, the 43-ft (13-m)
schooner *Lucette* was attacked by
killer whales and sank in 60 seconds.
Dougal Robertson, a Scot, and his wife
and four children were miles from any
shipping lanes when they took to the
9-ft (2.75-m) fiberglass dinghy towing
an inflatable rubber raft.

They had emergency rations for only
three days, and no maps, compass, or
instruments of any kind. The rubber
raft could not withstand the pounding
of the 20-ft (6-m) waves and sank,
forcing the family of six to cram
themselves into the tiny dinghy.

For 37 days, the family battled
against the savage seas, marauding
sharks, unquenchable thirst,
starvation, and exhaustion. They were
adrift in the vastness of the Pacific
and it was a wonderful mixture of a
mother's emotional courage and a
father's strong love and
determination that kept them going.
Miraculously, they were picked up by
a Japanese fishing boat more than a
month after their boat sank.

RESCUES
AT SEA

RESCUES AT SEA

The sea is a treacherous and unpredictable environment and it is not simply in the wide expanses of the world's great oceans that mariners can find themselves in difficulties. Very often, experienced and inexperienced sailors alike find themselves in difficulties in our inshore waters.

If you ever find yourself in a difficult situation in the sea, it is very likely going to be a brave band of men and women called the Coast Guard, lifeguard, or lifeboat service who come to your aid.

They are selfless and courageous and every time they are called out, they put their own lives on the line to save others from the overwhelming and capricious power of the elements.

When the call comes, these people are ready to serve regardless of whether it is a youngster cut off by the incoming tide or a large vessel that is stricken and sinking at sea.

The following extracts from actual incident reports from both the US Coast Guard and the British Maritime and Coast Guard Agency give you some idea of just how diverse and sometimes perilous their jobs can be.

MISSING KAYAKER

In April 2000, Lance Elizie, 20, and David Buck, 19, of Washington, North Carolina, began a four-day expedition that involved kayaking, camping, and hiking on North Carolina's Outer Banks. The pair began their trip in sea kayaks from Cedar Island at one PM on Thursday and they planned to arrive at a designated point on Portsmouth Island, 2.5 miles (4 km) farther north, later that afternoon.

However, the two kayakers were separated by 25–40-knot winds while en route to Portsmouth Island. Buck became stranded on a shoal, but Elizie finally made it to Portsmouth Island, although not to the predesignated spot.

Keeping a cool head, Lance Elizie called his wife on his cell phone, and she, in turn, called the Coast Guard. Elizie was soon picked up by the National Park Service and the search for Buck began in earnest.

After a cold and anxious wait, the Coast Guard helicopter eventually spotted Buck signaling with his flashlight, and he was airlifted to safety.

CHAPTER SIX

NEAR DROWNING

At just before seven PM on June 24, 2001, Swansea Coast Guards received an emergency call reporting five children cut off by the tide at Pembrey Harbour, near Llanelli, Wales.

The children, all from six to 12 years of age, had been walking out on a sand spit at Cefn Sidan at low water when they realized that the incoming tide was rapidly cutting them off from the shore.

Swansea Coast Guards scrambled to the RAF rescue helicopter and launched the Burry Port inshore lifeboat, and tasked the Coast Guard to help from the shoreline.

As the lifeboat arrived on the scene, they found that four children had managed to wade back to shore but the fifth girl had nearly been swept away. Fortunately, her quick-thinking friend, now safely back onshore, managed to find a rescue torpedo buoy, which he had thrown to the girl. He was in the process of keeping her afloat and trying to pull her to the shore when help arrived. The girl, suffering from exhaustion, was taken to a hospital.

Sea Survivor's Tip

This is a good example of what can happen when walking across sand at low water, especially at spring tides. You should always be extremely careful and make certain that your return path remains both safe and dry. "Without a doubt, this fortunate girl owes her life to the quick thinking and aptitude of her young friend," adds Watch Manager Terry Baldwin.

BOY SAVES MOTHER

One Sunday evening in June 2000, a 27-year-old man, a woman, and her son went swimming from his boat off the coast of North Carolina. However, unnoticed by the swimmers, the boat started to drift away.

The seven-year-old boy was wearing a life jacket, and luckily he was able to reach Roanoke Island. He immediately reported the situation to Dare County 911. The Coast Guard was notified and a rescue boat was able to rescue the boy's mother from the water about a nautical mile and a half (2.75 km) off the northern tip of Roanoke Island.

Neither the man nor the woman was wearing a life jacket and, sadly, the search for the missing man was unsuccessful.

Sea Survivor's Tip

Always wear a buoyancy aid when playing or working on or near the water. Without a shadow of a doubt, this saves lives.

MOTHER AND DAUGHTER SWEPT INTO HARBOR

A group of four people were walking along a breakwater in April 2001 when the sea swept two of the four — a mother and daughter — into the water. The 34-year-old mother and her daughter were obviously suffering from cold shock as they tried to stay afloat in the chilly harbor waters. Another member of the group, a 19-year-old young man, jumped into the water to try to help them, while passersby threw life rings down to them.

The survivors were dragged through the harbor water to dry land and safety where an ambulance, alerted by the Coast Guard, was waiting to whisk them to the hospital. Even in that short time, both mother and child were suffering from hypothermia.

Sea Survivor's Tip

"Anyone walking along a breakwater has to be aware that they are built to calm the waters on the leeward side and provide shelter for craft in the harbor. But they can take a terrific battering from the sea at times, and our advice is always to be careful when walking on such constructions," states Ross Greenhill, Aberdeen Coast Guard Watch Officer.

BOYS "LOST AND FOUND"

A mystery was about to unfold in April 2001, when a call was received at Milford Haven Coast Guard from 13-year-old Luke Sperway. He said that two boys from an original party of six had become separated from the main party on a two-mile (3.25-km) coastal walk back to their camping site, and he feared for their safety.

Milford Haven Coast Guard immediately coordinated a search for the missing boys. During communications, Luke then admitted that, in fact, he and the three boys with him were also lost and couldn't find the right track home. So, the Coast Guard rescue team and lifeboat, now assisted by a police helicopter, began searching for all six boys.

PICKED UP

Soon, the original four boys were spotted and the inshore lifeboat picked them up and took them to the harbor to help with information about the two boys still missing.

The Coast Guard rescue team finally found the two remaining boys, Joel Sperway, 12, and Scott Jones, 14, who were both soaking wet and very cold. They told rescuers that when they found themselves cut off by the tide, they were backed up against cliffs and up to their chests in water. So, they decided to climb and, amazingly, made it safely to the top of the cliffs. They picked their way through fields and woodland until the rescue team eventually picked them up.

No one was seriously hurt, but all six boys were very cold and tired after their ordeal. The Coast Guard praised Luke's calm actions during the drama, and his detailed account of the journey taken and their surroundings meant all six boys were located before dark.

Sea Survivor's Tip
Coastline Safety

- Anyone wanting to climb cliffs must ensure they have the correct safety equipment and that they are well secured by safety lines.
- Check tide times before taking a cliff or shoreline walk.
- Tell someone the planned route and the time you should be expected back.
- If you are caught by rising tides, never climb higher than is necessary to remain safe, i.e., to be clear of the water.
- Make all attempts to draw attention to yourself.

REAL-LIFE BAYWATCH

One summer's day in the British seaside resort of Bournemouth the sea was very rough and so the red flags (which mean no swimming) were raised. There was a 2-ft (0.6-m) swell that was causing a riptide to run across the breakwaters and jetties on the beach.

Carl Draper, the lifeguard on duty that day, positioned himself on the concrete landing jetty to warn people of the dangers. A woman and child standing in the shallows were getting too close to this rather dangerous projection and, just as Carl was telling the woman to take care, a large wave came in and pulled the little girl from her mother's arms and swept her out to sea.

INSTANT REACTION

The lifeguard instantly threw himself into the water, but he was slammed against the jetty, and he immediately felt an intense stabbing pain in his leg, but his only thought was for the little girl.

Ignoring the pain, Carl swam out to the child who had now sunk below the waves. He dived down and got her. Then they were both pulled out to sea by the powerful riptide.

With only one working leg, Carl struggled to keep the two of them afloat. The girl, though semiconscious, clung around his neck and Carl used every last ounce of strength to kick sideways to get them out of the dangerous rip.

Eventually, he reached calmer water and managed to bring the girl back into the shallows. As soon as she was safe, he collapsed back into the water and allowed the pain from his leg to wash over him.

Another lifeguard came to his aid. The bone in Carl's leg was exposed and he was taken to a hospital with severe lacerations, and tendon and ligament damage. Initially, the doctor's prognosis was that Carl would never walk again without a cane, but he was determined to get back to the job he loved.

With great courage, Carl is now fully recovered. He can swim, walk, and surf but he can't run properly or carry heavy weights. He paid a high price to save a little girl's life, but he is certain it was worth it.

Sea Survivor's Tip

Never ignore the lifeguard's warning on the beach. If you see a red flag, it means "no swimming" for good reasons, so stay out of the water.

A HELPING HAND

It is not always the professionals who show up to lend a helping hand. Every sailor is aware of the perils of being at sea. The awesome power of the oceans means that no ship or sailor is completely safe. That's why when a distress signal is received, mariners of every nationality will go to great lengths, and, in some cases, put themselves at considerable risk to help fellow seamen. All sailors know that one day they, too, may be at the mercy of the cruel sea.

Our final story is a real tale of David and Goliath, only this time it's the big guy who comes to the aid of the little fella!

INVINCIBLE ODDS

In June 1994, the captain of a huge container ship called the *Tui Cakau III* overheard a distress call from a small yacht called *Destiny* that was disabled and drifting in the heart of a raging South Pacific storm.

Captain Hebden could tell from the one-way conversation he could hear between the search-and-rescue aircrew and the woman on board, called Paula, that they were in dire straits. Her husband, Dana, had broken ribs, a punctured lung, and a shattered leg, and he couldn't move from the cabin below. The mast had broken and they were at the mercy of the storm.

FEROCIOUS STORM

Even with all his years of experience, Captain Hebden was awed by the sheer ferocity of the storm. From his bridge on his vast container ship, some 50 ft (15 m) above the water level, he watched as huge waves crested over the top of his ship and some even over the bridge itself.

Despite the atrocious weather, the rescue plane got through and pinpointed the yacht's location, but they were unable to lift the desperate couple off the stricken boat. The *Tui Cakau* was their only hope.

The *Tui Cakau* reached the vicinity of the *Destiny* in the early hours of the morning, but Jim Hebden was worried that his huge freighter might steam right over the forlorn little boat because visibility was so poor. It would be hard enough to hold a 7,000-ton (6,350 t metric) cargo ship alongside a 45-ft (14-m) yacht in calm conditions but in a raging storm, it was near to impossible, but he had to try.

EXTREME BRAVERY

Out of desperation, the captain and his first mate hatched a simple plan to rescue the

American couple. Two of his crew would descend down the side of the *Tui Cakau* and jump onto the crippled yacht. They would go below and carry the injured man back onto the deck and they would then be lifted to safety.

It was a perilous plan and he could not order anyone to take on such a dangerous operation. However, two men volunteered immediately. Joeli Susu and Survuama Valagotavuivui, both Fijians, stood 6 ft 3 in (190 cm) tall and both were super-fit. But more than that, they were both courageous men.

Captain Hebden had been on duty for 24 hours but he knew he must concentrate — one slip and the couple would die. Fighting with the controls, his first rescue attempt brought the huge ship closer to *Destiny* but the approach was wrong and the side of the ship crashed into the little yacht's bow, smashing her pulpit. Paula was terrified as they were nearly sucked under the stern and into the propeller of the great ship but the *Tui Cakau* passed by without any further damage. The captain had to rethink his plan.

A LUCKY BREAK

Suddenly, the conditions changed and the wind dropped to a gale. Captain Hebden recognized his chance and grabbed it with both hands.

The *Tui Cakau* approached *Destiny* a second time, rising and plunging in the swell. Men stood ready with a rocket to fire a line over *Destiny* while

Paula got ready to catch it to make her little boat secure. Meanwhile, the two rescuers stood waiting for the order to jump. Using all his piloting skills, Captain Hebden held the ship steady but nothing could prevent the two ships from colliding with a sickening crash.

The life raft containing Susu and Valagotavuivui was lowered down, and before she knew what was happening, the big Fijian Joeli Susu had jumped out and grabbed Paula and tried to put her in the life raft. But at that point, the rope holding the two vessels together snapped and Paula could only grab the wet companion net hanging down the side of the container ship as a huge gulf yawned below her with a frenzied sea at the bottom.

As the angry waves tried to claim her, a pair of strong hands gripped her from above and pulled her into the raft. It was Valagotavuivui, the second Fijian volunteer. They were quickly hauled up to the deck of the ship and safety.

TWO REMAIN

But that left Susu and the injured Dana on the crippled yacht. The crew sent more lines over to secure *Destiny* closer to the larger ship and, once again, Valagotavuivui descended to help.

In excruciating pain, Dana was unable to use the ladder, so an ancient canvas stretcher was sent down to carry him up from the cabin to the deck of the little yacht. As the *Destiny* pitched and rolled time after time, the two rescuers were knocked off their feet, either by the storm or by the two ships crashing together.

They persevered and lines were tied around the stretcher — strong hands started to pull Dana upward, but as the *Tui Cakau* rolled, he would swing far out and then crash back into the freighter's steel sides, sending pain shooting through his body.

Finally, Dana was on deck and his two rescuers managed to clamber up the cargo nets to safety. Captain Hebden had done a magnificent job against all the odds and the crew of the search-and-rescue aircraft still circling above cheered at the news of the successful rescue!

However, these brave and exhausted men could not rest on their laurels — there was another yacht in peril 80 miles (128 km) to the south, and the *Tui Cakau* was needed once again.

SAVING
LIVES

SAVING LIVES

There are several medical emergencies that commonly afflict survivors at sea and a little bit of first aid and survival know-how on your part could be enough to prevent these potential problems from turning into a disaster.

A cool head and clear thinking is what's called for when dealing with medical emergencies and you're just the person for the job. So take a close look at the following ideas for treatment and prevention of typical health problems at sea, and then I'm sure you'll be well able to cope with any emergencies that may arise if you find yourself cast adrift.

INJURIES OR ILLNESS?

Medical problems at sea tend to fall into two main categories. First, injuries sustained when your aircraft ditches into the water or when you abandon ship. These can range from cuts and bruises to burns or broken bones. The second group of problems arise from being in a life raft for a long time and these vary depending on whether you find yourself drifting in a hot or cold climate.

NASTY INJURIES

Ditching in turbulent seas is a precarious business and you'll be lucky to get away without a serious injury. At least you know what you're doing when you jump into the water but you can bet your bottom dollar some others are less informed, so you may be needed to administer some first aid.

CUTS AND ABRASIONS

Do you go weak at the knees at the sight of blood? Well, you're not alone. I've known hard-bitten war heroes who feel faint when they see a drop of the red stuff. But the important thing is that they overcome their fear to help others, and so can you.

SEVERE BLEEDING

In many cases, after a boating accident or a plane crash, survivors suffer severe cuts and abrasions, and you have to act quickly — particularly if you're in shark-infested waters.

≋ Remove or cut the casualty's clothing to expose the wound and then, using a pad, cover the wound. Press firmly on the pad with your fingers or the palm of your hand.

≋ Lay the casualty down on the floor of the life raft and keep the bleeding part above the level of her heart.

≋ Apply a sterile dressing (if available) over the original pad and bandage firmly in place. Don't worry if blood seeps through, just bandage another pad on top but make sure it's not too tight — check it at intervals and loosen if necessary.

Sea Survivor's Tip

If someone has fallen badly when leaving the ship or hit wreckage in the water, they might have broken a bone that will need setting once they get to a hospital. In the meantime, you can help by supporting the affected part of the body above and below the break, perhaps resting it on padding (something like a towel or the side of the life raft), and keep it as steady as possible in a comfortable position.

BURNS

Shipwreck survivors sometimes sustain serious burns from ignited oil spilled from the sinking ship. Burns are a particularly nasty injury and your quick actions can definitely make a difference to the aftereffects of a burn.

≋ Cool the burn down by pouring cold sea-water over it or, if safe, holding it in the water for at least ten minutes.

≋ Remove any restrictions, such as clothing or jewelry, from the burn area before it starts to swell.

≋ Cover the burn and surrounding area with a sterile dressing or, failing that, a clean piece of material.

≋ If the burn is large or deep, treat the casualty for shock.

CHAPTER SEVEN

Sea Survivor's Tip

- Don't apply lotions, ointment, or butter to a burn.
- Try not to touch the injured area and don't burst any blisters.
- Never remove anything sticking to the burn.

PROTECTION FROM THE ELEMENTS

Sun, sea, and sand may be a great combination when you're on your vacation, but put them together when you're adrift in an open boat and you've got a recipe for some very painful conditions.

In hot climates, the best health protection is prevention, so rig up some shade if at all possible, and if provided, use sunscreen during the day.

HEATSTROKE

This is the most serious result of overexposure to the sun and it's very unpleasant. In fact, if you don't get your temperature down, it can even result in brain damage or death. You can spot heatstroke by the following symptoms: hot, dry skin; a flushed and feverish face without sweating; high temperature; racing pulse; severe headache; vomiting; unconsciousness.

SEA SURVIVOR'S GUIDE

≋ The most important thing is to get the casualty into the shade and raise the head and shoulders slightly.

≋ Keep his or her clothing dampened with seawater.

≋ Fan them to bring their body temperature down.

≋ When conscious, let the patient sip as much water as you can spare.

Sea Survivor's Tip

Sun blindness is a very painful condition, caused by the glare of the sun reflected from the water. If possible, wear sunglasses or protective headgear. If not available, improvise eyeshades by cutting slits in cardboard or using some other blindfold. Darken the area around the eyes to reduce the glare, if possible.

SEAWATER SORES

As you can see, I recommend wetting a patient's clothes in seawater to cool them down, but this is something of a double-edged sword because constant exposure to seawater can produce body rashes and boils that may turn septic. If seawater gets into tiny cuts and abrasions, these, too, will turn septic.

These seawater sores have to be drained and cleaned with freshwater, if available. If you have antiseptic in the first-aid kit, use this for treatment. The only other solution is to make sure you wash both your body and your clothes during a downpour to prevent seawater sores from forming.

Fact File
It may seem like a joke, but real sunburn with blistering as opposed to a deep tan is a very real health risk. If more than two-thirds of the body is affected, it can prove fatal. Get out of the sun and protect your body from further exposure. Cover blisters with a dressing but don't burst them.

HYPOTHERMIA

If you pull a fellow survivor from a cold sea into your life raft, there's a good chance he or she will be well on the way to suffering from hypothermia. In this case, you should:

≋ Take off their wet clothing.

≋ Replace with spare, dry clothing. If none is available, wring out the wet clothes and replace.

≋ Use the body warmth of other survivors while you're sorting out the clothing to keep him or her warm.

≋ Wrap the patient in a foil survival blanket to prevent further heat loss. An ordinary blanket is the next-best thing if there's no survival blanket.

≋ If the life raft is open, try to shelter the patient from the wind either by a makeshift windbreak or using your own body.

≋ Give the patient high-calorie rations, such as chocolate (now that's what I call being a good Samaritan!).

SICK AS A DOG

Finally, all of you who feel seasick on a ferry please raise your hands. Well, imagine feeling or being sick day in and day out. Not a nice thought, is it? Seasickness is very common in small boats because the motion of the raft in the open seas is very pronounced. Unfortunately, once one survivor starts to throw up, then the others tend to follow suit soon after, making the raft an unpleasant and smelly environment for everyone. Worse still, continued vomiting causes the body to dehydrate and severe seasickness has caused tough men and women to want to die.

If there are seasickness tablets in the first-aid kit, take them without delay. If room permits, sufferers should lay flat in the bottom of the raft with the eyes shut as this sometimes prevents the feelings of nausea. Swimming alongside the raft is also effective but be vigilant — sharks can smell vomit from miles away.

Sea Survivor's Tip

If someone is sick in your life raft, quickly wash away the vomit with seawater to prevent the sight and smell of it from causing others to retch.

WHAT
IF . . . ?

WHAT IF . . . ?

I'll let you in on a little secret. If there's one thing I hate it's a smart aleck! It's so easy to say "I told you so..." after the event or to shout sound advice at contestants and competitors in extreme events from the comfort of the spectators' stand or an armchair in front of the TV. But, as anyone will tell you who has actually taken part in a tough competition or a real-life drama, it's much harder to make the right decisions when you're on the spot and under pressure. Anyone can be wise after the event.

That is why the military and emergency services around the world practice, practice, practice survival-and-rescue techniques time and time again. It's true that you can't plan for every eventuality, but getting into a certain way of thinking and rehearsing for some given situations can help to prepare you for the real thing. So, in our own small way, that's what we're going to do now.

I'm going to give you a few hypothetical situations and you're going to think about the way in which you would deal with them. Give it some serious thought, weigh every bit of information, and then come up with your plan. As a matter of interest, I'll then give you an idea of what I might do in the same situation and we'll compare notes.

So, put on your thinking caps, stay alert, and let's get going.

MAYDAY, MAYDAY . . . WE'RE SINKING

Your ship is passing through the North Atlantic Ocean when a fire breaks out in the galley. It quickly spreads to the rest of the ship, and the captain gives the order to abandon ship. Unfortunately, the fire is so fierce that you cannot get to the life rafts on the starboard side. However, there are two on the port side that are thrown into the water.

You are one of the last to jump into the water. The first life raft is full, so you and the remaining survivors swim to the second life raft. Disaster. It has inflated upside down in the water and you are left swimming next to it. Just to make matters worse, one of your fellow crewmates, who has been in the water longer than you, is gibbering from the cold and you can see that hypothermia is beginning to set in.

You are starting to feel numb in the freezing waters, too, and, as if this were not enough to contend with, a storm is mounting and the waves are getting rougher and bigger! What on Earth are you going to do?

SEA SURVIVOR'S SOLUTION

Phew, I'm exhausted after all that excitement and playing around with death! So, what cunning plan did you come up with? I guess a few of you might have swum underneath to see what could be done. I hope none of you punctured a hole in the top to get in or you'd be signing your own death warrant.

But did some of you decide to sit on the top? Not a bad idea — at least it gets you out of the icy waters for a moment, but you're simply putting off the inevitable. After all, this solution offers you no protection from the elements and all your survival packs and signaling equipment are still inaccessible. It could only be an interim measure.

So raise your hands if you had the bright idea of righting the raft. Well done. But do you know how you might go about it? In truth, it can be incredibly tricky until you get the knack — take it from a man who shivered for ages in icy waters because he couldn't master the technique straightaway. For anyone who has tried to get the sail of a windsurfer out of the water, you'll have a rough idea of what I mean. It's a tricky mix of strength and balance. So, just for the record, here's the theory, anyway.

RIGHTING A LIFE RAFT

You will need persistence, determination, and good balance if you are to get the raft upright. This is absolutely crucial if you are to survive in icy seas or to escape a gory end in shark-infested waters.

This apparently simple task is not too much of a problem in a training exercise scenario but in a storm, these lifesavers can be extremely difficult to right.

So, keep a cool head and allow the strongest person nearest the raft to attempt the following procedure:

- Find the pull rope on the raft.
- Pull yourself up into a kneeling position on the edge of the raft.

- Brace yourself by pulling backward on the rope and stand up. Easy on a still pond but not so simple on a choppy or churning sea!

- Keep your feet on the edge of the raft and fall back into the water. The opposite side of the raft should lift.

- Keep pulling on the rope while in the water. Once the suction with the water is broken, it should come over without too much difficulty — famous last words.

Fact File
Jet pilots who eject over the sea are equipped with a one-person survival raft. This contains all the equipment you might find in a larger multi-person raft but it can only accommodate one person, lying down. In fact, it looks a bit like a Day-Glo floating coffin but believe me, it is a lifesaver.

DANGERS FROM THE DEEP

The following scenario is everyone's worst nightmare . . . but you'd be surprised. As in all things, there is something you can do to help yourself. Can you figure out what it might be?

You are traveling in a small five-seater plane over the coast of Central America when a seagull flies into the engine. The pilot valiantly struggles to control your light aircraft, but it is impossible and you plummet toward the shimmering blue waters below.

Miraculously, you and your best friend manage to get out of the sinking wreckage of the plane, but both of you are slightly injured in the crash — you have a badly bruised left arm and he has a gash on his right leg. Unfortunately, you have no life raft.

One of the many cays (islands) lies within swimming distance but you have to get through the surf to get to dry land and, worse still, there are sharks patrolling just off the beach where the bottom drops off sharply.

You decide to chance it and swim ashore when, without warning, a shark "bumps" you (this is a very common shark tactic — it circles and bumps you before attacking). Any ideas on how to get out of this mess?

CHAPTER EIGHT

SEA SURVIVOR'S SOLUTION

This is a little tricky, but your situation does not have to be as hopeless as it at first seems. I'm sure some of you came up with the solution of saying your prayers, which isn't such a bad idea, but you can actually do something to help yourself as well.

Sharks are predators and they usually only continue with an attack if they are pretty sure they have an advantage. If you can retaliate, it shows the shark that you are not defenseless and it may decide to look for an easier meal elsewhere.

So the answer here is to fight back. Hit it as hard and as often as you can.

For those of you who came up with this plan of action, did you say punch it on the nose? Well, it is something of an old wives' tale that you should go for the nose. A shark's nose is not especially sensitive — in fact, you can inflict more damage by going for the eyes or gills. These areas are more sensitive to pain than any others and a sharp, jabbing action is most effective.

Use anything you have on hand — a water bottle, camera, harpoon, and, worst-case scenario, even your fist.

Your first thought should have been to stop your friend's bleeding since this will undoubtedly attract the sharks.

Bind up the wound with any material that comes to hand — if necessary, take off your T-shirt and use that to stanch the flow.

And finally, did you have the presence of mind to pull the survival pack from the plane when you evacuated? If so, you should have rummaged through the kit for some shark repellent before you set off.

You simply pour the liquid onto the surface of the water and allow the stain to spread around you — then make sure you keep within it. This stuff is highly distasteful to sharks and should keep them

away until the lifeboat can pick you up.

Sea Survivor's Tip

Avoiding Attack

- Stay out of the water after dusk and at night because sharks are more active at these times and can find you easier than you can spot them.

- Take off any watches, jewelry, or shiny objects since these reflect light, which a shark may mistake for the sheen of fish scales.

- Swim smoothly and silently without splashing — breaststroke is best.

- Keep in a group if possible — sharks will always single out an individual.

- Keep bodily fluids from the water. So, no blood, urine, feces, or vomit, all of which attract sharks (i.e., never mind that you're petrified, don't pee in the water!).

• Sharks are inquisitive and will show an interest in anything strange — if they show themselves they may just be curious and will probably swim away again.

• Despite what you see in films, sharks do not chomp their way through boats or leap out of the water to gobble you up whole. So, if in a lifeboat, remain calm and keep your limbs inside — well, there's no sense in taking unnecessary chances.

• Scuba divers, surfers, and body-boarders are at most risk when they lie on the surface because, from the depths, they resemble a shark's usual food, i.e., seals, etc. So, avoid loitering.

• Finally, although sharks do attack humans, we should keep our fears in perspective. For example, in the United States, you are 30 times more likely to die by being struck by lightning than by a shark attack.

Fact File
Shark Attacks

There are 300 species of shark but only 27 of these pose a threat to humans. Of the 27 who attack humans, the three who are known to repeatedly attack humans are the great white shark, the tiger shark, and the bull shark.

The largest predatory shark is the great white, growing to more than 21 ft (6.5 m) and weighing up to 3.5 tons (3,200 kg).

About 50 shark attacks are reported each year, but hundreds more probably take place in remote parts of the world and are never reported (see Amazing Escape on page 102).

Fact File
Amazing Escape

In February 2001, Mark Butler, a 40-year-old teacher was surfing off the Gold Coast of Australia when he was attacked by a 6-ft (1.8-m) shark. Mark didn't see the shark coming and he only realized what was happening when the shark bit into his leg and started to shake him like a rag doll in the water. Luckily, the shark let go and swam away!

With remarkable presence of mind, Mark took the leg strap from his surfboard and used it as a tourniquet on his bleeding leg and then started the arduous task of swimming in to shore. The sea was full of blood and all the time, he was frightened that the shark would return to finish him off.

After what seemed like an eternity (can you imagine?), Mark reached the shore and staggered up the cliff path. He then had to stumble a quarter of a mile (0.4 km) to find help – how determined is that?

Finally, Mark was taken by air ambulance to a hospital, where he received 180 stitches in his left leg. A narrow escape I'd say, wouldn't you?

WHERE AM I?

In the dead of night, you are awoken by the order to abandon ship. You grab a couple of personal belongings and, together with rest of the crew, you launch the lifeboat, just in time to see your mother ship sink without a trace to the bottom of the sea.

The lifeboat is well equipped with rations, water, and signaling devices but, for some inexplicable reason, all navigational equipment is missing. You know that you have enough rations to survive for many days. However, since a distress call was not sent out giving your position before the ship sank, and because you are a long way from normal shipping lanes, you know you have to try to find land yourselves rather than await rescue. You know your position and you know where the nearest land lies, but how the heck are you going to find your way to it?

SEA SURVIVOR'S SOLUTION

So, any ideas as to how to find your way back to dry land? I'm sure you were resourceful enough to come up with navigating by the natural elements, and, in this case, that would be the stars or the moon.

It is always a hard choice whether to stay put or to travel. Nonetheless, given the fact that you had good provisions, you were unable to signal any information before sinking, and rescuers will not know your position, and there's little likelihood of passing ships, you've probably made the right decision to move. So, how do you go about it?

NAVIGATING BY STARS

In the Northern Hemisphere, look for Polaris, also known as the Pole Star or North Star, because it remains static in the sky above the North Pole. So, if you can find Polaris, you have a good idea of which way is due north.

To find Polaris, look out for the constellation known as the Big Dipper, also called the Plough. It's made up of seven stars and the two stars at the end, farthest from the handle, point toward Polaris.

In the Southern Hemisphere, look for the Southern Cross, which points to true south. The Southern Star is found close to the dark area of the Milky Way stripe, at the end of an imaginary line drawn between two stars of the Southern Cross.

Studying the stars is always interesting, but in a survival situation it could just save your life.

BY THE LIGHT OF THE SILVERY MOON

On a clear night, you can also use the moon to help you navigate — it's not overly accurate but it's a useful rough guide. Both waxing and waning quarter moons can be used.

≋ **Draw an imaginary line through the horns of the moon down to the horizon.**

≋ **The point where it touches gives a rough indication of south, if you're in the Northern Hemisphere; north, if you are in the Southern Hemisphere.**

Sea Survivor's Tip
NEVER set off if you don't know your
own location.

≋ Cumulus clouds (fluffy white ones) in a clear sky suggest land. In tropical seas, look at the clouds. If they have a greenish tinge to the underside, this could be produced by the sun's reflection from shallow water over coral reefs and it's known in the trade as "lagoon glare."

Fact File
Is Land Nearby?
You can often tell if land is nearby, even if you can't actually see it, by a number of telltale signs.

≋ Pieces of driftwood, coconuts, or drifting vegetation are all indicators that land is nearby, although these can be carried across oceans on occasion.

≋ Don't get your hopes up if you see a lone bird, but if you see a bunch of them, you can surmise that land is not too far away. Very few seabirds sleep on water and most stay within 100 miles (160 km) of the coast — if you can hear continuous bird cries, then land cannot be that far away. Watch the direction of their flight — seabirds usually fly away from land before noon and return in late afternoon!

Sea Survivor's Tip

Your craft will move about 6–8 miles (9–13 km) a day simply due to the currents. However, you can use the wind to cover greater distances. Improvise a sail from cloth or clothing if you don't have one. Secure the top but simply hold the lower edge of your sail so that if a sudden gust comes along, you can release it before it capsizes your boat. If the wind is against your chosen direction, drop the sail, and devise a sea anchor to maintain your position.

≋ Watch the color of the water. If it is at all muddy with silt, then it has probably come from the estuary of a large river.

≋ If you spend a fair amount of time at sea, you get used to its movement. So, if you notice a change in the pattern or direction, it may be caused by the tides around an island.

Sea Survivor's Tip

If you find yourself in rough seas, stream the sea anchor from the bow (front) of your craft. This keeps the bow facing into the wind and should help to prevent capsizing. Keep low in the craft and, if you have to move, use a crouched position.

SEA
SURVIVOR'S
BRAIN-
TEASERS

SEA SURVIVOR'S BRAIN-TEASERS

We don't always take fire drills seriously when we have to practice at school and in the workplace (which is a bit dumb, really) but, on a ship, a fire poses an extremely grave threat. After all, if you burn your boats, so to speak, what are you left with? That's why you'll find that seamen take evacuation training exercises very seriously because knowing what to do in an emergency and what to take in the life rafts can mean the difference between being rescued in good shape and not being rescued at all.

So, how do you think you might react in the following perilous situation? Shall we see if you have any bright ideas on how to fathom out the solution to this rather puzzling seafaring disaster?

ADRIFT IN THE OCEAN

There's been a severe fire on your boat, and although you and the remaining three crew members managed to make it into a life raft unharmed, most of your supplies have been destroyed. You are left floating helplessly in the middle of the ocean. The only things that you've managed to salvage and that are left undamaged after the fire are:

Fishing kit
5-gallon (19-liter) can of water
Sextant (navigation tool)
Mosquito netting
Shaving mirror
Maps of the area
1 case of rations
Seat cushion (flotation device)
Small transistor radio — receiving only
2-gallon (8-liter) can oil/gas mixture
Shark repellent
20 sq ft (1.36 sq m) of opaque plastic
1/4 gallon (1 liter) of 160-proof rum
15 ft (4.5 m) of nylon rope
2 boxes of chocolate bars

WHAT TO DO

You must now rank the items in order of importance. In the table on the next page, number the items from one to 15 in descending order of importance. So, for example, if you think the radio is the most important item, put a one in the box next to it. And if the next-most important item is the fishing kit, put a two in the box next to fishing kit, and so on.

When you've completed the exercise, you can flip to the experts' verdict on page 112 and compare your answers.

So, best of luck — and may the best person win.

Items Undamaged by Fire

	Your order	Experts' order	Difference
Fishing kit	....	....	....
5-gallon (19-liter) can of water	....	....	....
Sextant (navigation tool)	....	....	....
Mosquito netting	....	....	....
Shaving mirror	....	....	....
Maps of the area	....	....	....
1 case of rations	....	....	....
Seat cushion (flotation device)	....	....	....
Small transistor radio — receiving only	....	....	....
2-gallon (8-liter) can oil/gas mixture	....	....	....
Shark repellent	....	....	....
20 sq ft (1.36 sq m) of opaque plastic	....	....	....
¼ gallon (1 liter) of 160-proof rum	....	....	....
15 ft (4.5 m) of nylon rope	....	....	....
2 boxes of chocolate bars	....	....	....

SOLUTION

So, how did you find that little conundrum? Do you think you got them in the right order? Well, let's find out what the experts think, shall we?

Correct Order

1. Shaving mirror. This is vital for signaling air-sea rescue.
2. 2-gallon (8-liter) can oil/gas mixture. Again, essential for signaling. The mixture floats so it could be ignited (once your raft is well clear, obviously).
3. 5-gallon (19-liter) can of water. Necessary to replenish loss from sweating and to keep you alive.
4. One case of rations. Provides basic nourishment.
5. 20 sq ft (1.36 sq m) of opaque plastic. This is ideal for collecting rainwater and to provide shelter.
6. 2 boxes of chocolate bars. This is a reserve food supply — so hands off!
7. Fishing kit. Ranked lower than the chocolate because a "bird in the hand is worth two in the bush." After all, there's no guarantee you'll catch any fish.
8. 15 ft (4.5 m) of nylon rope. Rope can be used to secure equipment to prevent it from falling overboard and is very versatile.
9. Seat cushion (flotation device). A lifesaver if someone falls overboard.
10. Shark repellent. Fairly obvious, I guess.
11. 1/4 gallon (1 liter) of 160-proof rum. Contains 80 percent alcohol — enough to serve as antiseptic for injuries but of little value otherwise. Whatever you do, don't drink alcohol in a survival situation — it dehydrates the body and makes your perilous situation even more serious.

CHAPTER NINE

12. Small transistor radio. Pay attention — it had no transmitting capabilities so although it may keep you and your friends entertained, it's not much use for anything else.

13. Maps of the area. These are worthless without navigational aids. It does not really matter where you are, but where the rescuers are.

14. Mosquito netting. There are no mosquitoes at sea.

15. Sextant. Once again, this is relatively useless without other essential navigational tools, such as tables and a chronometer.

Sea Survivor's Tip

The basic reason for ranking signaling devices above life-sustaining items such as food and water is that, if you cannot signal, there is almost no chance of being spotted and rescued.

As most rescues occur during the first 36 hours, food and water are less important during that period.

According to the experts, the basic supplies needed when a person is stranded mid-ocean are things that can attract attention and aid survival until the rescuers arrive. So, of primary importance are the shaving mirror and the two-gallon (8-liter) can of oil/gas mixture. These items could be used for signaling the air-sea rescue. Of secondary importance are items such as water and food.

SCORING

To get an idea of how well you fared, fill in the table with the experts' ordering and then figure out the difference between your scores and those of the experts.

Difference between your score and experts' score

0–20: Excellent — You'll be rescued within 24 hours.

21–30: Good — rescue within 36 hours. You're thirsty and need a shower.

31–40: Average — rescue within 60 hours. You're hungry, thirsty, and smelly.

41–50: Fair — rescue within 84 hours. You're sucking fish juice and looking hungrily at fellow raft mates.

Over 50: Poor — You're shark bait.

YOUR SEA
SURVIVOR'S
RATING

YOUR SEA SURVIVOR'S RATING

Well, my hearties, it's nearly time for us to bid a fond farewell to each other. But before we break into a rousing sea chanty and raise a glass of cider to each other's good health and future happiness, there's one thing left to do. Don't tell me you'd forgotten about the final questionnaire? You don't think you're getting off that lightly, do you? Men have walked the plank for less than that!

Anyway, before I get thoroughly carried away with my new role as Black Jack McBlack, the meanest, nastiest buccaneer who ever sailed the seven seas, we'd better get on with the quiz.

Find yourself a pencil and a quiet corner where you won't be disturbed and see how well you fare with this final survival test. If you've learned nothing else, you'll know to stay calm in an emergency by now . . . so if there's a question that's proving rather tough, simply flip back through the book because all the answers are hidden away in previous pages.

So, best of luck! It's the plank for the losers and a bottle of juice to the winners . . . sorry, I'm off again . . . just start without me!

1. What is the name of the solo around-the-world yacht race in which Tony Bullimore survived trapped in his capsized boat for three days?
A The Cowes Regatta
B The Vendée Globe
C The Fastnet Race
D The Sydney-Hobart

2. If you are forced to jump into the water you should:
A inflate your life jacket before you jump.
B inflate your life jacket once in the water.
C find some flaming oil on the surface and inflate your life jacket in the middle of it.
D Who needs a life jacket?

3. Research shows that if you are afloat in cold sea water (50°F/10°C) dressed only in light clothing, you will not survive for more than
A three hours.
B six hours.
C twelve hours.
D twenty-four hours.

4. Potable water is
A canned water.
B water for potted plants.
C drinkable water.
D water for carrying.

5. Your position can change by 50–80 miles (80–130km) per day by drifting in a life raft. You know that you stand a better chance of being picked up if you can stay put, having sent out an EPIRB (emergency position-indicating radio beacon) before your ship sank. So, what do you use?
A An anchor
B A buoy
C An oar
D A sea anchor

6. What is a quoit?

A A ring on a rope.
B The part of a rowing boat that you put your oars in.
C A flare.
D An emergency exit.

7. If you are finally lucky enough to sight land, you should look to beach your life raft

A on a shore protected by cliffs.
B on a beach with strong surf.
C on a muddy, root-tangled shore.
D on a pebbly or sandy beach.

8. The longest endurance record for survivors adrift at sea is

A 42 days.
B 92 days.
C 142 days.
D 365 days.

9. If a shark attacks you, you should retaliate by

A punching it on the nose.
B striking at the eyes and gills.
C punching it in the belly.
D grabbing its tail.

10. Three of the following four signs are good indications that you are nearing land but one is a fraud. Which is the odd one out?

A Cumulus clouds in a clear sky
B Pieces of driftwood
C Muddy water
D An albatross

11. One of your fellow survivors in the life raft feels horribly seasick. What should he do?
A Lie flat in the bottom of the raft with eyes shut.
B Sit up high and watch the horizon.
C Eat something greasy.
D Drink seawater.

12. You are shipwrecked in Arctic waters. You find land, but when you get out of your life raft, you find yourself on thin ice and — shock, horror — it's breaking up! Should you:
A run to thicker ice.
B lie flat and inch back to the boat.
C stand still.
D dance for joy.

ANSWERS

1b The Vendée Globe is a very tough single-handed around-the-world yacht race that takes place every three years and is always full of incidents. It was in the 1997 Vendée Globe that Bullimore had his brush with death. The other answers are all sailing events but of a different nature.

2b Never inflate your life jacket until you're in the water in case you get snagged up on something. And once in the water, choose your spot carefully — a burning sea is not a good place to find yourself. And if any of you dingbats chose answer (d) — no life jacket, then it's back to scrubbing the decks for you!

3a Three hours — that's all. It's not so very long, is it? So, if you have to abandon ship in cold waters, wear a decent amount of clothing. Funnily enough, in tropical waters, survivors report that sharks less frequently attacked those who were clothed than those who were naked — so the same rule applies here as well.

4c If water is potable then it is safe to drink. Of course, no one can guarantee what it will taste like — and believe me, water from a still is not the sweetest I've swallowed — but in an emergency it tastes like nectar!

5d Yep, dragging a sea anchor beneath your life raft will minimize your drift. Who said an anchor? Just how much rope have you got on your life raft? A buoy will just drift with you, I'm afraid, and you'd soon be exhausted if you tried to stay in one place by rowing.

6a You would throw a quoit to a survivor in the water (holding on to the other end of the rope, of course) to help them to your life raft. Funny word, isn't it?

7d A sandy or pebbly beach that is not being pummeled by huge surf or protected by hidden coral reefs (which can cut you to ribbons) is what you're after.

8c Amazingly, five fishermen from Costa Rica struggled in the immensity of the Pacific Ocean for an incredible 142 days, which is more than five months! Can you imagine?

9b The eyes and gills are the most vulnerable parts of a shark, so go for these areas first. Whacking it anywhere is better than doing nothing, but I don't suggest you grab a shark by the tail because, let's face it, you have to let go sometime and then . . .

10d A whole bunch of birds might signify land but a lone albatross doesn't mean a thing. This bird, also known as the "wandering albatross," which may give you a clue, can cover enormous distances, flying as far as 600 miles (965 km) in a day. They can even fly at night, so don't get your hopes up that you're saved if you see an albatross, or any other solitary bird for that matter.

11a There is no worse feeling than seasickness, but lying down can help. If you suffer from a bad and long-lasting bout of seasickness, you really do want to die. And that's precisely what you will do if you drink seawater, those of you who chose (d). How many times do I have to tell you? Some sailors swear by eating greasy food to cure seasickness but where you'd find a big fry-up on a life raft beats me.

12b If you lie flat, you spread your weight and so are in less danger of going through the ice. Running puts enormous pressure through each stride and is a recipe for disaster. Standing still — well, it's just a matter of time before something awful happens, whereas dancing for joy is plain lunacy!

Well, shiver me timbers, a full score, I'll wager — and if not, I bet it was near enough so I feel confident that you're now pretty well equipped to meet some of the dangers that the sea might throw at you.

However, there is not a sailor alive who would not tell you that the sea deserves respect. It can be an unbelievably beautiful, serene environment but the sea can change in a heartbeat into a savage, awesome, powerful foe that could smash your ship to smithereens in a second. Never court danger at sea — it would be foolhardy in the extreme.

You've probably noticed that none of the gallant survivors mentioned in this book put themselves at risk deliberately, so take heed and make sure you also take all the right precautions to enjoy our oceans safely.

I very much hope that one day you will have a chance to experience some of the same excitement and adventures that I have enjoyed at sea but make sure if you do so, that you do it in safe hands. There are some great sail-training organizations out there for young adventurers like yourself, so check one out if you want to feel the salty wind on your face and the thrill of a boat cutting through the sea.

So, until the next time we set out on a voyage together, best of luck and remember — a survivor is always learning. Now I'm off to find my land legs again!